OCCASIONAL PAPER SERIES 12

REVITALIZING HIGHER EDUCATION IN THE MUSLIM WORLD

•

A Case Study of the International Islamic University Malaysia (IIUM)

ABDULHAMID A. ABUSULAYMAN

THE INTERNATIONAL INSTITUTE OF ISLAMIC THOUGHT

LONDON · WASHINGTON

© The International Institute of Islamic Thought, 1428AH/2007CE

THE INTERNATIONAL INSTITUTE OF ISLAMIC THOUGHT
P.O. BOX 669, HERNDON, VA 20172, USA
WWW.IIIT.ORG

LONDON OFFICE
P.O. BOX 126, RICHMOND, SURREY TW9 2UD, UK
WWW.IIITUK.COM

ISBN 978-1-56564-430-4

Cover and Typesetting by Saddiq Ali
Printed in the United Kingdom by Cromwell Press

SERIES' EDITORS
DR. ANAS S. AL SHAIKH-ALI
SHIRAZ KHAN

CONTENTS

FOREWORD

EDUCATION IN THE MUSLIM WORLD IS FACING A CRISIS. What we see today is the cumulative effect of an absence of visionary leadership. This is compounded by a neglect of real investment in educational resources, lack of motivation on the part of educators, and a widespread loss of self-identity.

Some of these issues have been addressed by Muslim educators but in a piece meal fashion. Little attention however, has been paid to a comprehensive probe into the decline of educational standards across the Muslim world. Consequently, the combined scholastic productivity of Muslims remains at the lowest rung.

Education is one of the major building blocks of any nation. Economic progress and societal evolution are unthinkable without a functioning educational system. Similarly, national development policies cannot expect to be successful unless inextricably tied to a meaningful growth in the educational sector.

Education itself thrives in a free, democratic, and just society. However, the political landscape in the Muslim world is marred by repression. Unless we commit ourselves to remove bars to free inquiry there is little hope for an educational renaissance in our midst. Any initiative, therefore, to change the educational dynamics in the Muslim world and to bring it on par with world standards is commendable.

The establishment of the International Islamic University in Malaysia is one such ongoing experiment that shows signs of success. In this respect, AbdulHamid AbuSulayman is well suited to write on the topic of education, and specifically on the IIUM.

His distinguished service to the University and his eminent contributions to development of the intellectual capital in the Muslim world are commendable and make him an expert in this field.

The conceptual matrix of this institution of higher learning offers an arena for a critical reevaluation of Muslim approaches to education. On the other hand the intellectual incentives offered by the International Institute of Islamic Thought (IIIT) and material assistance from the Islamic Educational, Scientific and Cultural Organization (ISESCO) have played a pivotal role in the life of this institution. This stands to show that intra-Muslim cooperation, free of political interference, can produce tangible results.

Muslim scholarship constitutes an asset. We must therefore, devote ourselves to continually enhance its value not only for the Ummah but for the entire world to the ideals of a free, democratic, and just society.

ANWAR IBRAHIM
Former Deputy Prime Minister of Malaysia

REVITALIZING HIGHER EDUCATION IN THE MUSLIM WORLD

*AbdulHamid A. AbuSulayman**

THE PROBLEM

The remedy prescribed for a given problem is often inappropriate or insufficient for a complete resolution of a situation owing to an erroneous diagnosis or a defective analysis of the underlying causes. This applies in a real sense to the deficient diagnosis made for the underdevelopment of the Ummah (the Muslim nation), an ailment from which it has been suffering for several centuries. The ailment does not seem to have responded to any treatment since Abū Ḥāmid al-Ghazālī's (d. 1111) cry of alarm in *Tahāfut al-Falāsifah* [The Inconsistency of Philosophers] and an appeal for a cure in *Iḥyā' 'Ulūm al-Dīn* [Revival of Religious Disciplines]. One major reason for the failure of both diagnosis and treatment has been that the focus has hitherto concentrated on symptoms rather than underlying causes. As a result appearances alone have been targeted in addition to the distortion of the dominant concept of civilization and the inability of the approach used, limited as it is, to explore fundamental causes.

The Ummah has been suffering from a number of maladies that include underdevelopment, division, tyranny, and oppression, as well as injustice, poverty, ignorance, and disease. At the same time however, the Ummah yearns for power, unity, and justice. None of its hopes for political, economic, scientific, and technological

* President of the International Institute of Islamic Thought (IIIT), President of the Child Development Foundation (USA), former Rector of the International Islamic University Malaysia (IIUM), and former Secretary General of the World Assembly of Muslim Youth (WAMY).

development have been realized. Furthermore they still remain an elusive ideal, a mirage that always seems just out of reach over the horizon.

The Ummah and its people's desire to catch up with the developed world and enjoy high and truly human standards of living, education, and health is an aspiration that continues to be unfulfilled. There is agreement among major reformers that all these reforms are required. However, neither the awakening of the Muslim nation from its current lethargy can take place, nor its mission accomplished, without these reforms, particularly educational reform. It is also believed that these are reforms which address only the symptoms of deeper and more extensive causes. Unless Muslims adopt a bold and critical perspective to equip themselves with the appropriate tools of knowledge to identify these causes, the Ummah's failure to detect them will persist. It will continue to lack the ability to confront and overcome them, or to realize its legitimate cultural aims and demands and the practical reforms which it urgently needs.

All aspects of backwardness in the Ummah's history are but an expression of an inadequacy of performance. It is a disease caused by poor psychological motivation, stemming from a distorted vision and a defective approach. It results from distortions in the Ummah's cognitive and psychological makeup, which can be treated only when their true nature is discovered and they become the focus of the reform efforts by Muslims. Only then can the Muslim nation rid itself of hazy vision, poor motivation, and inadequate performance, which underlie its failure and backwardness in all aspects of life including politics, economics, science, and technology.

How could the Ummah have fallen seemingly irrevocably behind all others given the fact that it accounts for one-fifth of the human race, and covers an area extending from the Atlantic to the Pacific? The combined gross national product (GNP) of all Muslim countries is approximately US$1,100 billion, less than the GNP of France and about half that of Germany! It is also less than a quarter of the GNP of Japan, with a population of no more than 120 million, living in small scattered islands, poor in natural resources, with mountains covering more than three-fourths of the total area, and earthquakes and volcanoes plaguing both the land and the population.

One of the possible explanations for this tragic phenomenon is that Muslims seem to have lost their vision, the setting up of the highest objectives and the ethic of striving their utmost to achieve them. The current aspiration of the Ummah and its peoples seems to be no less than to survive with the least possible effort expended, envisaging no real future and no real ambition. They seem content to either simply produce basic materials using primitive methods or depend on foreign expertise and consumer-oriented assembly industries. Tons of metals and raw materials that are exported for a handful of dollars come back in the form of electronic and technological products worth millions of dollars. Why? Because the achievements of human beings are qualified by their performance, ability, and quality of thinking. The Muslim side seems seriously lacking in these virtues.

Today's Muslims are the descendants of the early Muslims (the Mission generation) and inheritors of Islamic civilization. The Muslim world has no shortage of natural resources. Its land is expansive and rich. Similarly, Muslims do not lack noble principles, values, and aims, for Islam has the lion's share of these qualities. Nevertheless, until Muslims delve deep into themselves and their history and scrutinize the cognitive and psychological distortion of their minds and souls, they will not be able to understand their backwardness and weakness. The ailment, in the final analysis, lies in the foundation of the Muslim intellectual structure with its attendant psychological effects that have led Muslims to the worst malady: performance inadequacy. It is an ailment that afflicts the patients wherever they go. It afflicts the Ummah in its public order, production, education, technology, protection of rights, and defense of the homeland. The only cure is to affect real and lasting change in oneself, that is, to change and reform one's very mind and soul, for: "God does not change the fortune of people unless they change inside" (13: 11).

EDUCATION

Reformers are right when they mobilize themselves to improve education, regarding it as one of the most important and the strongest building blocks of a nation. Unfortunately, due to their quantitative orientation, as in all other things, reformative action has remained superficial. It addresses appearances and is based on duplication and the imitation of all types of capable people. Thus, it blindly follows others in darkness, stumbling as it goes and where the road forks out, it does not know where to turn.

Undoubtedly, appropriate education and learning are the right foundations on which to build, for they are the two bases of dynamic human energy. Without them, neither power, production, nor achievement is possible. It is unfortunate, however, that reform movements in education and learning have essentially imitated the buildings and methods of others, including quantity and teaching aids. This is true even in the establishment of branches of foreign schools and universities. Thus, an examination of the prevailing conditions of education and learning in the Muslim world reveals a high concentration of what is termed "urban and technological," going too far in imitating all the latest fads of developed countries. The main interest of these reform efforts is in the importation of new machines, equipment, and systems. These efforts soon turn into "confusion and fabrication," guided only by "duplication and imitation." In its ideological essence, this approach is no different from the indulgence given to historical imitation and futile duplication that are perpetuated only by repetition and memorization.

Does it not seem odd that the reforms have failed to bear fruit? In fact throughout recent history they have not led the Ummah to the realization of a single objective, or a single goal. The lack of success and the loss of soul persist because of an enormous gap between the actual and the ideal, the assertions and the results. It should be understood that the implementation of reform of education and learning is not limited to tools, quantity, imported plans, blueprints, mechanisms, instruments, and equipment. Rather it involves a deep understanding of the essence of building blocks of humanity and humankind, a process that is a cultural, doctrine-based vision and a cognitive, intellectual, and scientific approach. This in-depth effort requires a particular ability such that appropriate tools are utilized, suitable quantity achieved, skills are developed to achieve goals, solve problems, and achieve reform and progress in political, economic, and technological arenas. The aim is triumph in the cultural race and delivery of the message.

WHERE TO BEGIN

The most important question facing Muslims at this point in time and on this particular issue is: Where does one begin? The answer is with self-reform. The beginning of Islamic reform lies in the reforming of every Muslim soul remedying the distortions in their ideological vision, cultural motivation, intellectual approach, and educational discourse. The tempestuous events that accompanied the Ummah's progression through the centuries and the cultural accretions of folk heritage left by various other nations are largely responsible for these distortions. They are akin to pebbles thrown at the cogwheels of Islam's cultural progress since its inception during the 6th Century. These impediments continually slowed its progress and reduced its impetus until eventually they stopped its motion altogether. It is a tragedy that the total number of trades and industries developed by the Ummah over many centuries has been of no avail. Today, it is a lifeless corpse, a neglected entity in the development of nations and civilizations suffering severe pain and continually lamenting its misfortune. More ominously, the Ummah has turned into a prey for its enemies.

How have things reached such a sorry state? How did it all begin? When did these distortions and impediments become such a serious impetus? It began in the century of conflict under the Umayyad rule, following the end of the era of the Prophet and the orthodox caliphate. During this period the performance of Islamic education and training slackened, favoritism and sectarianism flourished, and vestiges from the dark pre-Islamic cultures resurfaced in the midst of events which took place in rapid succession and posed formidable challenges. As a result, scholars who were striving to preserve the model embodied in the era of the Prophet were eventually isolated from government, politics, and public life. They were forced into a scholarly isolation, employed in issuing fatwas, handling individual affairs and matters of personal status, leading the prayers at the mosques, and urging worshippers, on Fridays and in mosque seminars, to observe high moral standards.

The exclusion and isolation of active scholars, upholders of the Islamic ideal, who are, in the final analysis, the Ummah's driving force, suffered from terrible consequences: the distortion of the comprehensive, cultural, ideological vision; the destruction of national leadership institutions and of the Ummah's educational future.

The comprehensive, civilized, doctrine-based Islamic vision is the creed of *tawhīd* (monotheism), of deputation, of belief in God and the Hereafter. It is a serious and positive creed that takes charity and reform as its purpose in this world ("Work for your life on earth as if you were to live forever, and work for your life in the Hereafter as if you were to die tomorrow!"). It turns a Muslim's life, in all its dimensions, into worship, *subjugating* it to the One True God. This vision serves as the conscience of the Ummah, stimulating it to righteous action that is useful in both this life and the Hereafter. It requires it to divide its time between invocation (of God's name) and jihad[1]. The invocation serves as an incentive to do righteous work useful for the Hereafter, that is, an incentive to spend all kinds of effort (jihad) in learning and in action. Thus, it is an incentive for the jihad for self-purification, seeking sustenance, pursuit of learning, endeavors at reconciliation, efforts to meet the needs of the deprived, advocacy in defense of faith, self-protection, defense of family and homeland, and defending the weak and the oppressed. This implies that a Muslim's life is a life of constant effort (jihad), whether in its private or public aspect, and whether it strives to meet individual or social needs. In all this, a

---

[1] Jihad: Literally, striving. Any earnest striving in the way of God, involving either earnest personal effort, material resources, or arms for righteousness and against evil, wrongdoing and oppression. Where it involves armed struggle, it must be for the defence of the Muslim community or a just war to protect even non-Muslims from evil, oppression and tyranny. [ed.]

Muslim seeks support by invoking God's Name, glorifying Him, reciting the Qur'an, praying, fasting, giving alms, performing Hajj, undertaking additional religious rites, and privately and publicly observing God's instructions.

> God has promised those of you who believe and do good that they will be His deputies on earth, the same as their predecessors were... (24: 55)

> Say, "My prayer, devotion, life, and death are to God, the Lord of all creatures." (6: 162)

> Those who strive for Our sake We will guide to Our right paths. God supports the righteous. (29: 69)

> Perform prayers, for prayers prevent lewdness and abomination. Invocation of God's Name is a greater duty. God knows what you do. (29: 45)

Meanwhile, the isolationist vision that came to be a prevailing feature of the elite Muslim scholars, was bound to have negative consequences that marginalized political governance, economic equity, social solidarity, performance of public office duties, and public institutions in general. It was bound to focus on the invocation of God's Name and religious ceremonies, as defined in Qur'anic terminology, calling them acts of worship and excluding other things although, from the Qur'an's perspective, a Muslim's whole life is a *worship*,[2] whether it is the invocation of God's Name or the pursuit of knowledge. The isolationist scholarly vision was thus a passive one giving little importance to the kind of jihad that took the form of action, activity, effort and earthly pursuits reducing it to mere procedures and contract rulings meant to regulate the transactions of people and affairs relating to their interests and means of livelihood.

This distortion of the comprehensive view, affected by the isolation of the elite scholars, was psychologically responsible, more than anything else, for the passivity that dominated the identity, goals, and collective functions of the Ummah in its

---

[2] While the Arabic words for worship, slavery, subjugation, and enslavement are derived from the same root, the concept of worship is derived from subjugation rather than enslavement, with the implication that by their free will, Muslims accept what is true and right. This for them is a source of pride and strength. ("Power belongs to God, to His Messenger, and to believers." – (63:8))

attitude toward life and its cultural and reformative purposes. It was no longer a positive, cultural vision that encouraged cultivation and labor, such that, even with the end of life approaching, the cultivator continued working when he had no expectation of living long enough to harvest the crop. This distortion of vision was certainly responsible for the death of consciousness and for the serious decline in important and creative endeavors in the life of the Ummah. It also bore principal responsibility for the corruption and division which seeped into public life; its passivity and poor psychological stimulation, and its defective cultural performance.

The scholarly isolation which men of learning and wisdom seemed mired in, produced in later days a one-dimensional vision, causing human knowledge and experience, as well as social changes, to retreat into a remote corner. Consequently knowledge became limited to textual and linguistic comprehension only. In the end, potential for renovation and interpretive judgment was ultimately stifled, with imitation and memorization becoming the dominant factors. Intellectual failure shielded itself with the sacredness of the text to overpower the will of the Ummah and subjected it, whatever the original intention, to the practices of dark ignorance and the clutches of promoters of self-interest.

Learning, science, and nearly all fields of human knowledge witnessed a decline in the centuries that followed the practice of imitation and decadence. The general education of the Ummah at large, and young people in particular became limited to modest elementary schools offering a simple and insignificant amount of education, parts of the Qur'an, basic principles of arithmetic, and just enough information for the common needs of daily life. The educational and instructional approaches used were defective, based on authoritarianism and punishment. This education was financed by parents with the little that they could afford to pay the unfortunate teacher who could find no better employment than the teaching profession. It was an educational system using methods and practices that became the target of criticism, censure, and of derision by many intellectuals and enlightened people when compared with the educational system offered to the children of the upper classes. Indeed, theirs was education of a different level, wider in scope than their poorer counterparts, and which included religious and literary studies. Students were well treated and not subjected to any abuse. This type of education included also the training given by government officials and upper class dignitaries to the tutors of their children at home. Nothing was added to these opposite poles of the educational system other than the existence of a few schools designed to train students to serve as a corps of prayer leaders, preachers, judges, and muftis.

With the distortion of the comprehensive ideological vision, the one-sidedness of knowledge, the barrenness of the cognitive approach, the setback of the religious discourse, and the tyranny of the political elite, the progress of the cultural spirit of Islam slowed down and the Ummah and its institutions experienced decline and decadence. People became afflicted with passivity and subservience, and the performance of individuals tended toward deficiency. All energy waned, and with it psychological incentives for excellent workmanship. It is those who are sympathetic and willing to work who devote themselves to and accept the burden of earnest and diligent work, whereas those who are fearful and reluctant are usually passive and content themselves with doing the minimum.

Performance inadequacy and poor motivation are still insurmountable obstacles to all efforts at reform. The Ummah has first of all to free itself from these shackles so that Islamic reform schemes can succeed, yield the desired results, and allow the Ummah to participate actively in modern civilization and the age of science and technology.

THE PLACE OF HIGHER EDUCATION
WITHIN ISLAMIC CULTURAL REFORM

Where does higher education stand within the Islamic cultural reform project? How do we revitalize and allow it to play the assigned roles: dissemination of knowledge and education, generation of new branches of learning, and the training of the personnel needed to meet the Ummah's present and future requirements? Since these are among the most important tasks and purposes of higher education, they go beyond the efforts to secure material equipment, administrative procedures, and the academic structures of schools that depend on the importation and imitation of cognitive patterns and educational and learning systems. Every cultural identity has its own starting point, objectives, values, and keys that release its latent potential. Any efforts that ignore these particular characteristics and do not address the potential energies of the Ummah's cultural identity will fail to awaken its conscience toward the necessary response and workmanship. Therefore, the Ummah will not be able to progress and take its proper place among nations unless higher education is revitalized and reformed, and the blights that have dominated it are removed.

AFFLICTIONS OF HIGHER EDUCATION IN MUSLIM COUNTRIES

The First Affliction is that of imitation and replication. The majority of higher education systems and philosophies in Muslim countries are Western in character, alien to the Ummah's conscience and cultural goals. Based on imitation and duplication, these systems fail to take into consideration the nature of Islamic civilization, as well as its special characteristics and values. These values are based on the principles of *tawḥīd* and deputation, the purposefulness and moral dimensions of existence, the unity of its foundations, and the complementarity of its material, spiritual, and moral – as well as its secular and eternal – dimensions. In Islamic civilization, gain, achievement, efficiency, and urbanization are not ends in them-selves, but rather tools for living and a spiritual means to something beyond, something more important. It lies in making the soul eligible for the immortality of the Hereafter with competence and charity, which express love of and subjugation to the One, the Most Just and Merciful.

The Second Affliction is the distortion of the comprehensive

Islamic vision, together with the blights, superstition, and charlatanism that have crept into the culture of Muslims bringing their development to a stop, and distorting their mentality, spoiling their knowledge, daily life practices, and educational methods. Moreover, it has drawn them away from the power derived from dependence on God and observance of divine examples in all their endeavors and life pursuits.

For these reasons and because of these afflictions, higher education in the Muslim World has failed to perform its role successfully, whether in religious or secular studies, humanities, or in science and technology. For the same reasons, higher education has not managed to disseminate knowledge, generate new disciplines of learning, and train creative and efficient personnel. The Ummah continues to be lost in its division and to live in the darkness of superstition, at the margins of human civilizational progress.

Reform and revitalization in higher education are essential elements for the Ummah's awakening and for the realization of its civilizational aspirations and the success of its global mission. Therefore, higher education reform has to begin at the roots by removing all the distortions afflicting it. One of the areas the reform must begin with is the Islamization of Knowledge, based on sound foundations.

Islamization of Knowledge calls for reforming our approach to education in a manner such that both divine and human sources are integrated into a powerful whole with Revealed knowledge providing a comprehensive spiritual and moral guidance in the sphere of human action and universal laws, and the scientific and technological knowledge as tools for that action. Thus, a complete mastery and proficiency of subject matter will result. This would remove the prevailing helplessness and lethargy, harness the dynamic faculties of thought, study, and research to focus on temperaments and occurrences, in applying the principles of reason and natural laws, and the guidance of revealed knowledge.

The Islamization of Knowledge – with its sound universal vision, integrated sources of knowledge, and observance of natural laws – will enlighten Muslim minds and enable them to explore the vast fields of science and knowledge, liberating them from superstitions and charlatan influences, as well as from the obstacles represented by inconsistencies, illusions, and perversities. In liberating minds, the Islamization of Knowledge will endow them with the ability to venture into the realms of science and knowledge with strength, confidence, and inventiveness. It will provide them with the equipment to seek reform, competence, and creativity. Thus, Muslims will acquire the capacity for serious ethical performance, and the ability to meet challenges, solve problems, reach desired ends, and achieve objectives.

A reformed Islamic vision and a sound intellectual approach are prerequisites for the refinement of culture and educational curricula. These in turn, are prerequisites for the affective structure of the soul, providing it with guidance for its movement and incentive for its performance. When this guidance and incentive become operative, there would be a wise and effective utilization of available tools and equipment, leading to the fulfillment of tasks and provision of needed materials, setting the Ummah's wheels back into motion, and stimulating its potential for ethical and creative production.

Therefore, if, after centuries of deviation and wandering, the Muslim world wishes to set the reform agenda on the right track, its priorities have to be reflected in an educational reform plan. It must put quality before quantity, content before facilities, and curricula before instruments. However, each of these items must be given its due place in both function and purpose, without any conflict or failure.

A balance in quality and quantity, content and facilities, is characteristic of nations with performance skills. With culture, education, and learning, these nations express their identities and their civilizational foundations. This balance originates in their innate energy and the performance incentives within their structures. They place cultural and educational affairs, and the skilled training of human beings, at the top of their lists of priorities, providing their citizens with all the available resources required to ensure that they become the instruments to achieve the goals and objectives of those nations. Backward nations, on the other hand, are wont to imitate and replicate. Their educational systems fail to express their basic principles, features, and civilizational particularity; and they are rather an artificial combination, both in vision and orientation. Educational needs and requirements are placed at the bottom of their lists of concerns, and these are the first to suffer the effects of scarcity when a crisis occurs and helplessness and failure are compounded. Yet, it is a known fact that energy renewal and improvement of performance depend mainly on the quality of the culture and on the improvement of educational curricula.

THE ISLAMIZATION OF KNOWLEDGE: A LIVING EXPERIMENT IN REVITALIZING HIGHER EDUCATION

The Islamization of Knowledge is a project that concerns knowledge, learning, and education. It originated and developed in the minds and conscience of a group of Muslims who were aware of the spirit and cultural power that lay behind the greatness of Islamic civilization, and knowing the role they themselves could play in elevating human civilization as a whole to new horizons.

Characterized by a high measure of sophistication, wisdom, and proficiency from the scholarly and professional experience of its members, the group knew how effective Islamic values were in securing the Ummah an eminent position in human history and how this served as a starting point for other nations that later developed their cultures and achieved their aims.

Advocating and strongly believing in the Islamization of Knowledge, the group envisioned the combining of the disciplines of Islamic history and culture with both contemporary culture and science, in other words, a remarkably intellectual integration of knowledge fusing the disciplines of revealed knowledge and those of human and technological sciences.

The integration of knowledge advocated by the group is reflected in the early writings of some of its members, in works such as *The Islamic Theory of Economics: Philosophy and Contemporary Means* (1960), and in the group's efforts to establish a major Islamic cultural society, the Muslim Students Association in the USA, in 1963. This particular association grew and became a nucleus for important Islamic institutions sponsored by the Islamization of Knowledge movement, the most important (from an intellectual perspective), being the Association of Muslim Social Scientists in the United States and Canada (established in 1972), the International Institute of Islamic Thought (IIIT, 1981), and the Child Development Foundation (1999).

The rationale of the Islamization of Knowledge is the conviction that the Ummah's crisis and performance deficiencies lie first and foremost in the distortions that have plagued Islamic thought, disrupting its unity of knowledge, and transforming it into a stagnant textual body of knowledge. These distortions in turn also marginalized the role of human knowledge within the structure and performance of Islamic thought. They destroyed the seeds of human disciplines, which had started to sprout in the secondary origins of the principles and concepts of Islamic jurisprudence. The result was the decline of the Ummah's institutions, unity, and ruling regimes. Moreover, religious discourse came to develop an intimidating character, which, with the widespread phenomenon of intellectual impotence and political despotism, pushed the Ummah into a passive role, causing it to lose its creative, cultural energy, and suffer humiliation and backwardness. We know a reluctant and scared person does not make any effort beyond the minimum required, whereas generosity, dedication, and creativity are characteristics of a willing and warm-hearted person.

The Islamization of Knowledge is a plan to reformulate Islamic thought, using as its starting point Islamic beliefs and Islam's humanitarian, global, and civilizational principles based on *tawḥīd* and deputation. The plan aims at recapturing the positive, comprehensive Islamic vision, with a view to reforming the approach to education, built on an indissoluble integration of divine and human knowledge. The plan addresses the reality of human life on earth with the aim of realizing the purposes of Islamic Law –

namely, conciliation and welfare – and observes the principles of reason and the divine laws of the universe. It thus, provides the necessary tools to purify and refine Islamic culture and remove the distortions, and the superstition, charlatanism, impurities, and illusions that have infiltrated it. Ultimately, it will provide sound educational and cultural inputs to reform the mental and psychological constitution of Muslim individuals and of the Ummah and raise generations endowed with strength, ability, and productivity.

The IIIT regards its basic task to alert intellectuals and educators, regardless of their specializations and orientations, to the nature of the crisis and aspects of educational reform. This will consequently allow them to also shoulder their responsibility in cultural reforms and development, work towards the improvement and validation of educational curricula, and the stimulation of the Ummah's potential energy so that its progress may be improved.

Towards this end the IIIT has cooperated with the Muslim intellectual elites throughout the world in joint efforts that have provided Muslim thinkers and scholars with platforms for dialog and significant scholastic contribution. The Institute's efforts have lead to the establishment of centers and institutions, organisation of conferences and symposia, and the publication of books and periodicals in Arabic, English, and other languages spoken both in the Muslim world and elsewhere. It has also sponsored joint activities with all concerned with the question of intellectual and educational reform.

All this represents a hope, a promise, and a serious issue of great significance, offered for academic and scholarly discussion, to explore and apply in the reconstruction of the Ummah's thought and its civilizational foundations. This is one of the most important foundations for the creation of conditions necessary for the awakening of the Ummah, to activate its potential energy, and to carry out its civilizational enterprise in the service of humanity.

THE ISLAMIZATION OF KNOWLEDGE EXPERIMENT AT THE INTERNATIONAL ISLAMIC UNIVERSITY OF MALAYSIA (IIUM)

In 1956, Malaysia became an independent country and started to feel its way toward building itself as a new state. The Malaysian leadership recognized the role Islam could play in stimulating the energy potential of its Muslim population and, influenced by the First Conference on Islamic Education, held in Makkah in 1977, founded the International Islamic University (IIUM) in Kuala Lumpur, Malaysia in 1984 after an international agreement with the Organization of the Islamic Conference (OIC). The IIUM, which has since grown from strength to strength, was meant to be part of a system of international Islamic universities, as envisioned by the OIC, to focus, within their overall curricula, on Islamic culture.

Malaysia's leaders recognized the nature of the constructive, civilizational, and reformative thought contributed by the IIIT which held one of its international conferences, on the Islamization of Knowledge and Reform of the Cognitive System, in Kuala Lumpur in 1984. Anwar Ibrahim, the Malaysian Minister of Education at the time, had had a close relationship with the Institute since the time he served as a member of the General Secretariat of the World Assembly of Muslim Youth in Riyadh. Therefore, in 1988, he invited the IIIT to support the fledgling university, with a 1,000 number student population. The Ministry requested the Institute to second one of its members to put the concepts of the Islamization of Knowledge into a university educational plan that would serve Islam and support the reform and development efforts in Malaysia.

The Institute, represented by one of its thinkers with experience in organization and university education, took charge of the University between 1988–1999, during which time both its physical and academic construction were completed. The curricula of its colleges covered all the disciplines of Islamic studies and human sciences, in addition to architecture, engineering, and medicine. The university had two campuses, as well as an additional campus for preparatory courses in Arabic and English. It also offered complementary courses for those students whose educational systems failed in some aspects to meet their needs and the University's requirements, such as students from the former Soviet Union and students of general education who had only had eleven years of pre-college schooling.

BODY AND SOUL

The planning of the two campuses – the main in Kuala Lumpur and the medical campus in Kuantan, consisting of the School of Medicine and the Faculty of Science – was carefully thought out and designed to express, both ideologically and physically, concepts of the Islamization of Knowledge and its premises. These concepts and foundations are particularly embodied in the Kuala Lumpur campus, the construction of which was completed in 2006, excluding certain affiliate facilities and services.

The University today has an enrolment of some 15,000 students, and its achievements are not merely a matter of creation and innovation in curricula and programs. It is, in its own right, one of the most elegant campuses in the world, expressed in the structure and beauty of its Islamic architecture and efficiency of performance in the best of Islamic values.

The mosque is situated in the middle of the campus and represents its spiritual center, with student and staff traffic continuously flowing around its walls in all directions. It is an important arena for cultural and spiritual activities. The grounds of the campus and the way its facilities have been designed to connect with each other, provide a spirit of cultural and social intimacy. Moreover, the locations of the student hostels and recreational and sports facilities carefully observe Islamic criteria, ensuring, in addition to performance efficiency, the privacy and freedom of each of the two sexes. The objective has always been to uphold Islamic standards of morality in the relations between the sexes and to respond to all their psychological, social, cultural, recreational, and sports needs in the best manner.

DISCIPLINES OF ISLAMIC REVEALED KNOWLEDGE
AND THE HUMAN SCIENCES

The core of the IIUM system has always been its academic and educational curriculum. The syllabus embodies the goals of the Islamization of Knowledge, having been developed to remedy intellectual and methodological distortions, to build a mechanism for cultural refinement, and rebuilding the new generations of this Ummah, both psychologically and educationally.

The most important task on the agenda of the IIUM administration was to confront the distortion of knowledge and methodology and to recruit alternative, educated work groups, characterized by unity of thought, knowledge and thoroughness of approach. The most important field for this alternative academic approach was that of Islamic studies and the humanities.

To achieve this, the Faculty of Islamic Revealed Knowledge and the Human Sciences was established. The largest college, it comprised all specializations in Islamic studies and the social and human sciences. For professional reasons, the disciplines of economics, administrative studies, and law were excluded, although their syllabi were to have the same purpose and objectives.

The cornerstone of the academic system of this college – aspiring to realize the goal of the unity of Islamic knowledge, reform of methods of thought, and the training of alternative educated groups of leaders and professionals – was the development of a double-major, credit-hour system.

Under this double-major system, every student specializing in Islamic studies had to choose a cognate major in one of the human sciences. Likewise, any student majoring in the humanities had to have Islamic studies as a cognate major. Students who were willing to study for one additional year could fulfill the requirements of a second bachelor's degree in the cognate major. The university encouraged this option. These students would finally have two university degrees, one in Islamic studies and the other in the social science subject that they had originally chosen as a cognate major.

This duality of knowledge and specialization is a system which provides students with not only a wide scope of knowledge, complementary in orientation and tools, and a superior comprehension of the dimensions of spiritual, ethical, and social life. It also trains them in particular (the analogy method in Islamic study) and general (the methods of the social sciences) methodological complementarity with various study tools of these methods. This is a very important methodological element in the integrated cultivation of student mentality and of future performance skills.

This system of study serves to expand the students' intellectual capabilities to include the general, social aspects (social studies) in addition to the personal and spiritual aspect (religious and ethical studies). With these expanded capabilities, students acquire the intellectual tools to interact with the soul and the psychological and cognitive spirit of the Ummah. In addition, the dual system opens the door to a wider range of employment for students. Consequently, the skills of these young people are utilized and their dignity is safeguarded, particularly in countries which have Muslim minorities. Or, in poor Muslim countries, where employment opportunities are scarce, especially in religious services.

With a degree in social sciences – coupled with a mastery of the English language (the language of instruction of technical courses), and Arabic, (the language of instruction in religious subjects) – graduates have the ability to work in any appropriate civil field they wish. They are qualified for employment in the civil service, in the teaching profession, or in private business. They do not have to enter, as often is the case with Islamic studies graduates from some Islamic universities, a profession which does not suit their abilities and training. Graduates qualified in both Islamic and social studies have, by any standard, a more thorough knowledge and a wider range of thinking, comprehension, performance, and efficiency than others.

Under this system, the University admits graduates from one of the major universities into its postgraduate programs if they meet its requirements, which call for a good background in the subjects of revealed knowledge, as well as any field of human science in which the student has majored.

For example, students who want to study any of the disciplines of Islamic Law at M.A. or Ph.D. level have the chance to do so after completing the requirements of that discipline. These include mastering Arabic and completing the required number of basic courses in Islamic studies. On the other hand, if the applicants are graduates of a department of Islamic studies, they have to meet the basic requirements of a social studies subject and English, in addition to Arabic, which they are supposed to have already mastered.

Although the International Institute of Islamic Thought had offered this idea to some universities in the Muslim world, they later abandoned the system and reverted to the single-major system in their postgraduate Islamic studies. The reason was that these universities could not develop a good program of social studies or effective courses of Arabic for non-native speakers. However, by reducing the period of study, they gave quantity a greater importance over quality.

The system at IIUM has been successful for several reasons. Most important is the large number of graduates of the University itself, with Islamic and social studies majors, who seek admission into postgraduate studies at the University.

In addition, the IIUM has developed its program of Arabic for non-native speakers into a series of courses that ranks as the best in that field. Moreover, graduates of other universities are highly interested in being admitted to the IIUM's postgraduate program. The fact that mastering Arabic and English is a prerequisite for their admission makes those who know only one or neither of the two languages work hard in their home countries to catch up with or join the University preparatory program at their own expense. Thus, the IIUM does not have a shortage of applicants for its postgraduate programs. In fact, the demand is higher than it can accommodate. This allows those programs, with the integration of knowledge and the methods of investigation and research they offer, to fill the intellectual arena with people who have experience and knowledge covering the various disciplines of natural and human sciences from an Islamic perspective based on the principles, values, and purposes of Islam.

The development of course assignments in each discipline, taught from an Islamic perspective, has been regularly monitored. These courses cover the whole syllabus that students of the same level study at secular universities, with the addition of a critical Islamic evaluation and a survey of any Islamic viewpoints that have materialized in the field in question. With this approach, the Islamic perspective suddenly has a voice, is elevated in its own right, and provides a considerable academic contribution which enriches the educational disciplines. It is envisaged that with time, this enrichment will prove its validity and credibility. It will grow in various fields to make a real contribution, serving the Ummah's interests in cognitive development. The quality of graduates that would emerge, whether in their performance levels or their achievement, will also offer Islamic perspectives in intellectual and scientific spheres.

Several academic courses and fields of study that relate to the Ummah's concerns, needs, and perspective have been designed. These are courses in religion, philosophy, law, the humanities, economics, and administration. They are listed in the University Bulletin for undergraduate and postgraduate studies as part of the curricula of various colleges and departments.

In this context, one can mention Western Studies, in particular, which began as a part specialization and gradually developed into a major subject. It is now a department that offers a conceptually accurate and perceptive study of Western history, thought, and culture. The graduates of this department are specialists that help the Muslim mentality to understand the West itself, as well as its cultural and human contributions and transgressions. This can be useful in dialog and interaction with the West. It contributes to the fulfillment of Islamic reform aspirations and to the development of relations with the West. These ought to be based on active and constructive cooperation that overcomes grievances, grudges, and acts of aggression that are encouraged by the backwardness, weakness, and division of the Muslim World. The Ummah's interaction with the achievements of modern civilization and societies can thus be based on objective understanding and methodological foundations. The Muslim mind can then confront this civilization as a system that has its own characteristics, foundations, and own purposes, with the understanding that interaction with it is aimed at positive, mutual, and fertile cooperation, for the good of the human race and its global civilization.

In physics, engineering, and similar fields, the Islamization of Knowledge does not deal with scientific facts per se but as to how these are put to use for the service of humanity. Differences and variations, however, come from the methods used in dealing with, utilizing, and benefiting from, these facts and laws. This includes the ethical standards observed in using them, whether for progress or destruction, for seeking benefit or causing harm. All these things are concerns of the Islamic faith, covered by its culture, science philosophy, and ethics of research and professional practice. In this regard, there are different schools of thought, attitudes, purposes, and cultures. The Islamic perspective functions to ameliorate and guide, distinguishing good from evil, benefit from harm, and humanitarian concerns from barbaric actions, and restoring the spirituality and nobility of life and its purposes.

Another aspect that relates to natural sciences and their study is an awareness of the history and contributions of the Ummah. This is in order to establish historical justice and free it from the Western bias, and to enhance self-confidence among Muslims with scientific knowledge. This can serve as a stimulation to resume the process and as a means to learn the lessons of how the progress in the past was impeded, how the way was lost, and how the Muslim mind deviated from its seriousness and objectivity into a world of illusion, superstition, and backwardness.

What is important in formulating the mechanism of the Islamization of Knowledge approach is the concept of program development. This means continuity and persistant application of effort to achieve civilizational ends. It is a continuing process of development and urgency that enriches thought and culture and meets the needs and conditions of live, developing societies. This process starts from firm ethical points and leads to benign and explicit ends and achievements.

The development of the content and quality of study courses, based on the principles of the Islamization of Knowledge, never stops. It gains momentum with continual revision in light of the experience gained and the interaction with the needs of the Ummah and of society. By supporting the ever renewing cognitive store of students and expanding their horizons, the University equips them with potential educational and psychological abilities that make many corporations and government agencies seek to employ only IIUM graduates. These graduates are characterized by competence, high moral standards, seriousness, education, skills, and potential. Many officials and visitors from other Muslim countries request the IIUM to help them train students in order to acquire graduates of equally outstanding quality and high competence, both educationally and professionally.

LANGUAGES AND ARABIZATION

Languages play a vital role in efficient performance. While thought and curricula are the content, languages are the performance tools. Thus, the more efficient the tools of performance are, the greater is the likelihood of success.

IIUM has given considerable attention to the language question to guarantee excellent and efficient performance of graduates and to provide opportunities for learning, productivity, and communication between them and their working environments. Therefore, in addition to their mother tongues, students are trained in two international languages: Arabic and English. This, under the prevailing conditions in the Muslim World, gives them access to source materials, whether Islamic, educational, or technological.

In teaching Arabic and English, the IIUM provides teaching aids, following the most up-to-date international methods and using Islamic content and guidance. Arabic serves as the language of Islamic religious learning and for effective communication between Muslims. English serves – in the early twenty-first century when scientific and technological resources in Arabic and other languages of the Muslim World are still scarce and inadequate – as the language of instruction in modern scientific and technological courses. Thus, the students are in a position to communicate and interact with the intellectual, cultural, scientific, and political elite in most Muslim countries at this stage. With the two languages, Arabic and English, IIUM graduates are qualified to play an active role in their countries. With their combined intellectual, educational, and effective abilities, they can contribute to the development of thought and areas of study in their societies and their spheres of action.

It is hoped that educational and scientific Islamic institutions, both regional and international, will address the language dilemma of the Ummah to find a radical solution. This predicament has been contributing to the cultural failing and political division of the Ummah. Unless scientific and educational activities are carried out in the native language of a nation, its culture and education are bound to suffer. Education will be limited to an inadequate acquisition by a minority that masters foreign, international languages in which resources are available. The most important of these now is English, which is most often a second language for students and, consequently, does not allow them to be creative, for creativity can only occur in the mother tongue.

The Ummah can acquire a significant position in learning and culture only by using a widespread international language, rich in scientific terminology, particularly in physics and technology. This requirement can only be met by using the language of the Qur'an, which serves as an effective bond for all Muslim peoples. Even an illiterate Muslim has a reasonable knowledge of Arabic from the Qur'an. If this knowledge is systematically nurtured, those people will have a cherished international first language, common to all of them, which gives them access to scientific and technological materials and enriches their culture and their conscience at the lowest cost.

Owing to their love for the Qur'an, Muslim peoples will not hesitate to adopt Arabic language as their religious, educational, and scientific first language, in addition to their local tongues and colloquial dialects, as long as it is available to them and they feel no need to learn any other language. What Arabs and Muslims have to do is to contemplate their own experience in Arabization and that of the advanced nations with their diligent and prompt translation of every new scientific addition, particularly in physics and technology. Such is the case in Japan, Russia, China, Germany, the United States, and other countries.

One of the most important areas of priority for translation into Arabic is the scientific and technological periodicals, which are the channel through which new contributions in all fields make their first appearance. The translated version should be readily available at educational and scientific institutions and public libraries, because technology moves fast in those countries that have reached scientific superiority.

The cost of establishing institutions for the translation, publication, and efficient distribution of new editions appearing in the periodicals of science and other disciplines would be less than the cost of major universities in many Muslim capitals. When scientific knowledge becomes available in Arabic, there will be much more demand for its learning and studying the religious, cultural, scientific, and technological materials available in it. Translation will become a business and assignments will be completed in record time. Using Arabic as the language of school and university instruction will be easy and effective, and will repudiate all objections against its usage. Usually, these arguments are advanced not against the language, which has a remarkable ability of expression in all its forms, but against the failure to reinforce it with new scientific materials, as is done with international languages and the languages of active contemporary nations.

With the flow of scientific translations, the problem of terminology will automatically disappear. Standard terminology will be promoted by publication and usage. This promotion can be supported by establishing a language academy with contributions from all the current academies, making a unified effort to keep up with the activities of translation, Arabization and standard terminology, free from local bias and isolationist tendencies, which have destructive motives and which reflect, or respond to, foreign and colonial interests.

LANGUAGE SIMPLIFICATION:
GRAMMAR AND SPELLING

It is high time for Arabic academies to make greater efforts to simplify Arabic spelling and grammar, making the maintenance of sound and accurate comprehension of the Qur'an a working criterion, which allows also for the comprehension and preservation of the Arab/Muslim heritage. With that guaranteed, proper learning and using the language can be made easier in an age in which the scope of knowledge has greatly expanded and education is the right of everyone, not only that of privileged groups and specialists.

Because of the greater ability one gains from electronic devices in dealing with a language, discovering its mysteries, and surmounting its difficulties, it is possible now to acquire an analytical understanding of all cases and issues of the language that has not been so feasible in the past. Therefore, it is hoped that the efforts of linguists will solve many complexities of the language, particularly those of spelling that have no benefit and add nothing significant.

One example of spelling difficulty which, in this education-for-all age, seems unnecessary is the various and complicated methods of writing a glottal stop *(hamzah)*, depending on its type, position[3], and the vowel preceding it. No other sound has such complex rules for spelling, which, difficult and complex as they are, cause many people to make mistakes in writing, even when they are able to figure out its type. Rather than help people spell correctly when they write, the rules seem to have no other purpose than to prove people's ignorance of them.

A similar case is that of the soft *alif* at the end of three-letter words, which has two methods of writing depending on the root from which the word is derived, where the letter is originally either *wāw or yā*, and this determines how the *alif* is written. When one is

---

[3] By type is meant whether it is /a/, /u/, or /i/. By position is meant whether it occurs at the beginning, middle, or end of a word.

unaware of the origin of the *alif*, one is likely to make a mistake in writing it, or, at best, may write it correctly by imitation, without knowing the reason for the spelling. Whatever the case, this is an example of rules that bring no special benefit, and there is no need to burden the language learners with them. They only make spelling difficult and exhaust the memory of students.

These are only examples, and there are many other cases that need to be simplified or standardized, such as a past tense verb ending with an *alif* and different cases of present tense verbs and verbs in the imperative mood ending with vowels. In some of these cases, a silent *alif* is added after a *wāw* with which the verb ends, while no such silent *alif* is added at the end of plural nouns ending with *wāw*. A third example is the omission of the long *alif* sound in certain words (demonstrative pronouns in particular). There are many other cases.

It is important to reconsider Arabic grammar formulae and methods of teaching. Admittedly, it is important to distinguish between the subject and the object of a verb, particularly when the object precedes the subject, because failure to distinguish them may affect one's understanding of the intended meaning. Distinction by the final inflection is not possible with names that end with long vowels (such as Munā and Lailā), and only sentence order and/or context can serve to distinguish between subject and object. Inflections, however, do not serve to distinguish between an adjective and an adverb. No inflection tells us whether a noun has a certain quality or is in a certain condition; after all, both cases are matters of description. Therefore, these problems call for a thorough reconsideration of many grammatical rules. The linguistic reform movement should pay special attention to sentence structure and to context, both of which influence comprehension, without becoming involved in formalities, traditions, and professionalism related to meaning in formulating and teaching Arabic grammar. It is imperative to simplify classical Arabic and facilitate its appropriate and effective usage by Muslim learners wherein education is no longer a privilege for the upper classes or for specialists. Linguists in our age must make the effort to simplify the language and promote a more effective language performance, without affecting the basics necessary for understanding the Glorious Qur'an and comprehending its meaning, implications, and style. They should take into consideration that the various methods of language usage by Arabs, past and present, has neither affected their ability to communicate with one another, nor reduced their eloquence.

Although both the International Institute of Islamic Thought and IIUM are aware of the need to enrich Arabic and to put effort in giving it its proper place, this undertaking is beyond the capabilities of either. The most they have been able to achieve is making Arabic the language of instruction at the IIUM and to make source materials available for the Ummah's scholars and intellectual elite. The two institutions have also focused on the publication of journals and other periodicals in Arabic, as well as in English. The publication of intellectual and educational works and research papers in Arabic enriches the Ummah's knowledge and thought, and their publication in English serves as a global contemporary vehicle for communication with many nations and with the intellectual elite in many countries of the modern world.

It is important for concerned parties, official and non-official, charitable and commercial, local and international, to give special attention to scholarly and scientific translation, particularly the translation of major academic and scientific periodicals, into the language of the Qur'an, to enrich that language, and to make it eligible to be the scientific and educational first language of all Muslim peoples. The Islamic Educational Scientific and Cultural Organization (ISESCO), the Arab League Educational Cultural and Scientific Organization (ALECSO), governments of Muslim countries, and educational and research institutions throughout the Islamic World must cooperate and coordinate their efforts to bring this plan into existence and to ensure success for both the Ummah's civilizational goals and its aspirations for unity for the good of humanity.

We deceive ourselves when we dream that others will transfer science and technology to us because science and technology continue to develop with astounding speed. They can be mastered only by a person qualified to be productive and endowed with a scientific mentality, a creative ability, and a rich background. Therefore, the beginning must include better intellectual training for the Ummah's new generations and future personnel. With every new work published in science and technology, this, in turn will revitalize their energy, trigger their enthusiasm, reform approaches and methods of thought and education, and enrich their culture, especially the Arabic culture. Initially, this has to be done in the native languages of the various Muslim peoples, and later, according to a carefully drawn up plan, they can be unified culturally through the medium of the language of the Qur'an.

It is a very easy aim to achieve if the Ummah has the resolve and insight and she develops and utilizes all the tools that will allow her to be capable and productive and to revitalize her scientific and technological institutions and workers, with God's help.

CULTIVATION OF KNOWLEDGE AND
ENCOURAGEMENT OF RESEARCH

The cultivation of knowledge and encouragement of research undertakings are the other side of the coin in terms of actions required in the Islamization of Knowledge at IIUM.

It is true that undergraduate education at the University and its complementarity in all departments are crucial for training a work force with integrated knowledge and methodological skills and for creating a full range of inter-disciplinary and comparative studies. On the other hand, postgraduate studies, research by faculty members and graduate students, research center projects, the interaction of these projects with life and society, publication of scholarly and scientific writings and international periodicals, hosting academic seminars and meetings of faculty members, holding dialogs, discussing academic and scientific issues and concerns, exchange of views and expertise, co-sponsorship of symposia and conferences with academic and international institutions – all these matters have received utmost attention and backing at the IIUM. For this reason, and within a relatively short space of time, the University has become an academic and scientific platform and a beacon in religion, human sciences, medicine, and engineering education. Many symposia and conferences have been held there, covering various subjects of study.

From the very beginning, IIUM has offered an extensive post-graduate program offering M.A. and Ph.D. degrees in a number of areas of Islamic studies, human sciences, education, economics, law, and engineering. Library and laboratory facilities are provided, and channels of cooperation with various educational, scientific, and industrial institutions have been established. This policy and the willingness to provide all kinds of services, as well as cooperation and exchange with various parties with similar interests, have been productive and have yielded numerous research works by faculty members and graduate students. The University has been working at constantly improving the standard of these works and their orientation toward contributing to Islamic thought in meeting the Ummah's needs.

The IIUM Research Center, the Academic Council, and the latter's committees in various colleges have provided researchers with support and encouragement and sponsored their projects, in cooperation with educational, scientific, and industrial institutions, firms, and concerns. The University has implemented carefully prepared research plans to meet urgent needs. The teaching load of anyone demonstrating outstanding research skills in areas that meet the research priorities of IIUM and the Ummah is usually reduced. Sometimes, in case of certain research projects, it is waived altogether to allow the faculty members concerned to devote all their time to research. In order to serve integrated knowledge and the complementarity of curricula in student training, IIUM opens its doors, within the limits of research plans, to experts and specialists (outstanding judges and lawyers, successful business people, and experienced scientists). They are welcome for a full or part-time contribution, by participating in its teaching and research programs, offering consultations and advice, or serving on boards and committees that guide the University and upgrade its curricula and syllabi.

One of the research projects to which academicians were fully committed was the preparation of syllabi and textbooks and the construction of an educational organization plan for a model international Islamic school. This school was meant to be the nucleus of an Islamic school system covering all stages of general education from nursery school to secondary education. The system would be guided by Islamic concepts and vision and aim at providing children with wholesome, positive, and enlightened Islamic education. It would also develop in them a sound scientific and methodological mentality that was not tainted by deviations and distortions of superstition, charlatanism, and the residue of traditions inherited from ancient cultures. This school system would endeavor to reconstruct the concepts of family and the school education of students so that they would grow into honorable human beings with the creativity, initiative, and a constructive and reformative spirit that reflect the Islamic concept of deputation. At the culmination of the project, an all-level school was established, with a student body composed of the children of faculty members and any children from the general public that the school could accommodate. Although the project is still at an initial stage, the early projections of the system and curricula indicate a degree of success that encourages continued efforts toward the desired end.

One of the tasks of the research center and the office of its dean is to organize consultations and research projects by faculty members on behalf of, or in collaboration with, companies and establishments. Moreover, IIUM has developed a program for the publication of outstanding works written by faculty members. It also publishes a number of journals in English, some of which are specialized and published by various colleges and specialized research centers. An academic journal in Arabic called *al-Tajdīd* [Innovation] is also published. It observes the highest academic standards of objectivity and free intellectual expression, as always advocated by the University, as long as research and expression stem from a scholarly spirit and aim to serve Islam.

These efforts are complemented by the academic activities of all colleges and departments, such as, academic programs that include seminars, lectures, panel discussions, and conferences – domestic, regional, and international. A number of these conferences and meetings are organized annually in Islamic studies, the humanities, and physical science. The Islamization of Knowledge is the guiding principle for these activities devoted to the discussion of issues that concern the Ummah and development of knowledge from an Islamic perspective. Because of the seriousness and efficiency of IIUM activities, various universities and research centers inside and outside the country, as well as international institutions, have cooperated with the University. These include the International Institute of Islamic Thought, the Islamic Educational, Scientific, and Cultural Organization (ISESCO), and the Islamic Development Bank. The cooperation has positively augmented research efforts expanding research horizons and experience. IIUM publishes an annual book of completed and continuing research work by faculty members. Thus, IIUM's academic programs have proved their ability to encompass all the positive aspects of the contemporary spheres of science, with an Islamic spirit, vision, and cultural purpose. All this raises hopes for a prosperous civilizational future.

THE INTEGRATION OF ACADEMIC AND
EDUCATIONAL PERFORMANCE

It is established that the reform of curricula achieves an integration of knowledge and equips students with the cognitive bases that form the content of their minds and their methods of study. Meanwhile, related cultural pursuits and campus activities are of great importance in shaping the students' psyche and their future interaction with society.

The first resource that should be available to students within the university environment is sound general knowledge, remedying deficiencies in any areas that are needed to correct the distortions pervading Muslim societies. The courses and programs designed for this purpose are included in the general requirements program offered to students. This includes academic programs at university level and student affairs programs. They are intended to fill the gaps in students' background; enhance their spiritual, religious, cultural, and educational development; and to equip them with cultural aptitude, social and physical skills, and constructive energy. In spite of the intensive curriculum, the productivity of students is doubled and their comprehension capacity increases in an extraordinary manner.

The University requirements program is included in the curricula to provide students with an ideological, ethical, and cultural foundation, and thus to upgrade their education and knowledge. The program also aims at preparing students to play their social, leadership and professional roles. With this in mind, IIUM offers – in addition to courses in religious doctrine, ethics, and general education – a course on Family and Parenthood, which provides male and female students with the scientific, social, educational, and Islamic perspectives of the subject. The purpose is to lay the cornerstones of the basic social structure, the family, on a sound psycho-sociological Islamic foundation, and to equip young parents with the tools to follow educational methods and achieve the desired ends. This is an effort to produce citizens with spiritual and moral strength, objective mental capabilities, creative psychological potential, and feelings of dignity and self-confidence. Thus, future generations may have the necessary courage and initiative as human beings to succeed in their role of vicegerents and their mission of construction.

To serve the same purpose, IIUM offers a course in Creative Thinking and Problem Solving. The course promotes awareness of the nature of creative thinking, its psychological and educational foundations, and its scientific tools. Young people can thus be guided in developing their thought and performance and in raising their children on bases that allow the Ummah and its young generations to take part in the race for civilization building.

A course is entitled the Rise and the Fall of Civilizations. It is a University requirement because this Ummah was the heir to a

number of ancient civilizations and is now in a close race with
other civilizations. Young people need therefore to be equipped
with an encompassing civilizational and scientific perspective that
helps in the rationalization of programs for the desired civilizational
Islamic reform.

The University has introduced two postgraduate diplomas for
teacher training in Family and Parenthood and Creative Thinking
and Problem Solving. This allows the University to include courses
on these subjects in its basic requirements. For the same purpose, a
Student Affairs Office has been opened. It is one of the largest and
most important of the IIUM's offices. It has the task of releasing the
potential of students, fostering in them a brotherly and group spirit
and a sense of belonging to the Ummah. The Office provides a
wide range of activities and experience, cultural programs, free
education, and training in various skills. These programs bring all
the students and faculty members together as one big family. The
students comprise more than ninety-six nationalities and faculty
members more than forty. All of them are driven by a sense of
having a mission, a spirit of brotherhood, a feeling of true belonging, a sublime objective, and an awareness of the challenge.

The administration of IIUM, the management of services and
admissions, and all the staff of the administrative departments at
every level, from the lowest ranking official to the highest, including, leadership, are, according to the IIUM policy, considered
part of the University family and share in the educational responsibility. In fact, the educational role of the administrative staff may
be more influential since they serve as an example to the students,
who deal directly with them and feel their influence in their daily
study routine. They base their concepts and style of dealing with
others and with the society in general on the model and quality of
that interaction. Therefore, driven by an Islamic sense of mission,
IIUM makes every effort to maintain the dignity of its staff
members and meet their needs and those of their dependents. It
extends easy loans to them to help them build their future and
provides them and their family members with medical services and
children's nurseries. That is how the IIUM looks after its staff

members. By the same token, staff members are expected to treat students well, respect their dignity and the human nature with which God has honored every human being, take care of their needs, be always ready to help them and smoothly process any applications they submit, provide them with all possible services and counseling without complicating matters and disregarding their ethnic, linguistic, or religious identity. Muslims and non-Muslims are treated equally.

Experience tells us that with a sense of responsibility, solidarity, and joint interest based on justice, equity, equality, appreciation, encouragement, and respect, and with the provision of training and experience, as well as guidance and counseling, positive energy can produce a vast output of work smoothly and easily. The cost and energy needed for this work are much lower than that required by negative, wasted efforts spent in overcoming obstacles and in the conflict that prevails in organizations that have no clear objective, sense of mission, group interest, or sense of belonging. It is true, as demonstrated by experience, that achievement, progress, and success require great efforts, but impediments, conflict, and backwardness require in fact greater effort and toil. It is also clear that real poverty and want reside in the lack of vitality and the spirit rather than in resources.

PROMISING RESULTS

The Islamic spirit and mission common to all work approaches, together with the building of team spirit, are behind the great success achieved, within only one decade, by this remarkable academic edifice. These achievements are due to the Islamization of Knowledge plan and concepts and the creative curricula of the IIUM as well as the Islamic-style backing of the most cost-effective creative academic programs, installations, and facilities.

It is, therefore, not surprising that this outstanding edifice, based on the Islamization of Knowledge project and its civilizational foundations, is providing the Ummah with an outstanding work force in all fields. Nor is it surprising that its academic programs, systems, regulations, and cultural, social, and educational arrangements are a qualitative and quantitative step forward in higher education. It is a step that covers the range of experience and talents and the fields, concerns, and issues of research. It is a step forward in the scheme to revitalize higher education to serve the Ummah's civilizational aspirations, release the potential of scholars, activate latent capabilities and productivity, and meet the Ummah's spiritual, intellectual, and functional needs.

In their performance during this short period, IIUM students have proved that they have better capabilities than their counterparts who have graduated from other, well-established universities, and that they are often the winners in cultural and sports competitions, not only in Malaysia, but also in East Asian and Asian–African tournaments. They always hold leading positions at the Australasian level and in international cultural contests. In the 2000 international debate contest of college students, the IIUM team managed to be amongst the top ten teams, a first for a non-English-speaking country. In fact the team ranked seventh among hundreds of teams from major English-speaking universities around the world. Moreover, the IIUM male and female taekwondo teams are the champions of this sport in Malaysia. When the soccer team at the University had its own field at the new campus in 1998, it managed to win the Malaysian soccer tournament from a former team that had held the championship for three successive years. In the tournament, none of the university teams managed to score a single goal against the IIUM team.

Reports of the achievements of the graduates of this young university and of the high leadership positions they hold in their countries, which are closely followed by the administration and alumni society, are concrete evidence that its foundational logic is sound. It is the logic of the Islamization of Knowledge to revitalize higher education and serve the Ummah's civilizational aspirations. It is also apparent that the foundations of this logic are capable of stimulating civilizational energy latent in the Ummah with the least effort and at the lowest cost. Quantity then would turn into quality, scarcity into abundance, and cheap into precious and expensive. This has been the experience of live, alert nations and their active systems whose culture and educational programs activate the potential energy and productivity of their citizens. The IIUM experiment is, therefore, a pioneering endeavor that is worthy of consideration and contemplation. Many would benefit from the lessons that it teaches in developing and revitalizing higher education in the Muslim world to serve the Ummah's interests and civilizational aspirations.

RESOURCES AND FUNDING

The seriousness of the agenda, the steps it has taken, the ends and aims sought by the IIUM project, as well as the methodological reforms it has achieved, and the academic and educational policies it has drawn – all these have enabled the University to appeal to the conscience of activists and revive hopes in many hearts. Its founders have witnessed their hopes and ideals as embodied in the project come to life and witnessed success take shape in the form of strong, intelligent Muslims as models of human progress at both academic and civilizational level. Consequently, the necessity and validity to contribute financially and in other ways has been awakened. Individuals representing all strata of society – ordinary people, activists, officials from all over the Muslim world – have been visiting the University to see for themselves first hand its *modus operandi*, to learn as much as they can about it, and to offer advice, encouragement, and contributions.

Although the Malaysian government has undertaken to finance IIUM programs, establishments, and buildings, many international Islamic institutions and organizations have extended their contributions in financing campus buildings, scholarship funds, and international conferences in an unprecedented manner. Likewise, charities, business people, and other philanthropists have extended their financial assistance to the University and its scholarship fund. Thus, thousands of outstanding students of more than ninety-six nationalities, representing all the ethnic groups and cultures in the Muslim world and reflecting its future unity, are supported in their studies.

Contributions do not take a financial form only; interaction with the IIUM mission is also represented by the excellence of its human resources, individuals who have made sacrifices to join the faculty. They offer their knowledge and experience to students, thus supporting IIUM's academic and educational programs. The sacrifices have been made not only by many individuals, but also by universities and other educational and scientific institutions, which have released some of their outstanding faculty and staff members to help the University with its new programs and to contribute to its teaching and research efforts.

The financial and human resource support received by IIUM from the host country, the Malaysian people, and academic and scientific Islamic institutions and individuals from both within and outside Malaysia is an expression of the impact that this project has produced. It has touched the souls and consciences of all the people concerned, awakening in them the urge to give, activating charitable inclinations to serve the Ummah, and revitalizing the educational establishment through this University and its future promise to help reform Islamic thought, culture, and education through the Islamization of Knowledge.

This experiment teaches us important lessons about the stimulation of latent energies, the propensity to make liberal contributions, and the revitalization of the educational establishment as a basis to release the forces of the Islamic, civilizational reform initiative. These lessons should be applied, not wasted.

The experiment should be well comprehended, benefits should be reaped from it, and it should be developed, and utilized in other experiments to revitalize higher education institutions to serve the Ummah's future and its civilizational aspirations. It is hoped that ISESCO will finance research into this experiment and the IIUM campus as a creative Islamic model. This research should be made available to universities and other higher education institutions in Muslim countries.

THE FUTURE

An awareness of the dimensions of the Islamization of Knowledge project and its role in reforming the higher education establishment is an imperative. This, in turn, can reform the Ummah's intellectual and educational life. It is possible to upgrade the quality of education and research, and that of leaders and professional work forces on the premise that activates the Ummah's potential, touch the conscience of Muslims, set them in motion, rectify the distortion and damage done to the bulk of their culture and minds, and build a positive psyche.

Without an awareness about those in charge of higher education institutions and the administration of intellectual and educational policies, the revitalization of education and the consequent stimulation would not be possible. Otherwise, the higher education establishment will, for generations to come, continue to be a suffering invalid, as it is today and in the past. Against the international criteria and standards set by modern civilization, the education system will remain helpless. The work forces that graduate for employment will continue to have hazy thinking, a polluted culture, distorted programs, and limited ambition. They will aspire for nothing more than earning a livelihood, driven by their instinct for survival. They will be indifferent, regardless of how many imported devices and machines are made available to them. Although additions can be made to these most up-to-date machines, nothing better than what has been seen so far can be expected. After all, future conditions can be divined from past experience.

The hope entertained by the Islamization of Knowledge school is to be able to reach out and alert elite intellectuals, thinkers, educators, and all groups with Islamic thinking and perspective. These people have to bear their responsibility in intellectual and methodological reform in general, and the reform of higher education in particular, since that is the field from which emerge the elite and the academic, scholarly and professional work forces of the Ummah. The elite in question must undertake the necessary intellectual effort to purify and refine the Muslim culture removing all superstition, charlatanism, and outmoded forms of thought, and all else that is in conflict with objective thinking not based on rationalization and divine laws of nature.

This process is an important requirement for success. Since Muslims are expected to do their best and then depend on God, the elite must ground all matters in faith and belief, combined with their dependence on God's Will. They should fortify everything that supports and strengthens the inclusive Islamic outlook, the moral concept of deputation, and the constructive, civilized mentality. The Islamic literature needed for reforming educational curricula and for training parents and equipping them with an educational background should be made available. This is needed in order to raise a generation fit for the responsibilities of deputation and free from the dangers of a slave mentality; a generation characterized by purity and humility and the spirit of initiative and creativity. It is only parents, with the influence they have on the minds and consciences of young people, who can start the process of change. This makes parents – with their instinctive concern for their children's well-being and their willingness to sacrifice everything to serve their children's interests – the key to reform and change, based on the convictions nurtured in them by intellectuals and educators.

If we compare the scholarly, scientific, and educational studies by advanced nations and their thinkers and educators to educate parents, teachers, and community leaders with that of the Islamic thinkers, we will unearth one of the secrets underlying the Ummah's backwardness. After all, its civilizational aspiration has been lacking to the extent that Muslim children are neglected, and so is the literature needed to raise and educate them. In addition, the training of the Ummah's intellectual and professional work forces, by using the little that is available in Islamic culture and education, too is neglected. This is due to the lack of concern in the higher education establishment for an effective Islamic culture. It is their failure to play a role in revitalizing learning and knowledge and in training leaders and professional work forces to meet the

Ummah's needs. They must remove the distortions afflicting its thought, culture, and educational programs that prevent the Muslim mind from being effective, thus failing to stimulate its potential.

To have scientific and technological work forces in great numbers should not be an aim in itself. Instead, we should prepare these forces to serve the Ummah, meet its needs, and help fulfill its reformative and civilizational aspirations. This includes mastering their specializations with great proficiency, being productive and serious, and having the sense of responsibility that encourages better performance. The reform of education, the refinement of culture, and the pedagogical education of parents are some of the most important areas of the Islamic civilizational reform. The International Institute of Islamic Thought has been working to offer a model and an experiment that embodies its concepts and principles and which proves its validity through a successful release of the potential for young Muslims, the activation of their latent abilities, and proving the excellence of their performance. The International Islamic University in Malaysia has served as an experiment for the revitalization of higher education in the service of the Ummah. It is hoped that under the current conditions in South-East Asia, the University will thrive in its mission and serve as a model for other efforts to serve the Ummah with the revitalization of higher education and the reform of its foundations.

When this is achieved, higher education can, with God's permission, exploit the potentials of the Ummah and stimulate its leadership and educational and professional work forces to serve human civilization and guide its progress.